Zephyrs of the Heart

Duane L Herrmann

ISBN: 978-93-95224-06-2

First Edition: 2022
Rs. 200/-

Cyberwit.net
HIG 45 Kaushambi Kunj, Kalindipuram
Allahabad - 211011 (U.P.) India
http://www.cyberwit.net
Tel: +(91) 9415091004
E-mail: info@cyberwit.net

Printed at Vcore LLP.

"Endeavor your utmost to compose beautiful poems to be chanted with heavenly music; thus may their beauty affect the minds and impress the hearts of those who listen."

~ 'Abdu'l-Bahá

CONTENTS

OBSERVATIONAL

Standing on the prairie
sky all around,
the human speck
considers
the difference
between his puny form
and the vasty sky.
How can he presume
superiority? Yet
scripture says
the universe is enfolded
within the human form,
supreme apex
of Creation.
He realizes
the "real" universe
is that unseen realm
beyond this life.

OPEN the DOOR

Look within,
deep within
and we will find
Divine
standing, waiting
for us to open
the Door of our Heart
and welcome in
That Which Was
always within,
and our loneliness
will vanish.
For we are never alone
when we listen
to That Voice
speaking softly
within – waiting
for each of us.

LISTEN to the...

Grace of the world
can flow
to you, to me, when
we ourselves are still
enough to listen.
Slow Down.
Stop.
Pause a moment.
Hear the wind,
the leaves.
Is there a bird?
Let it sing to you,
follow its freedom
into the sky
above worries
since all will be well
in Creator's time
when that may be.

WARNING

Ruined shed,
still and low
falling pieces down.

Farm life ended,
dreams are dead and gone.
A single tree remains.

Desolation speaks
of hard times,
social imbalance...

"Complete regard should be given...
agriculture is endowed
with the first station."

Words of wisdom...
unheeded,
society dies.

Wind bends dead grass and weeds
air is cold and dry
a year and life are gone.

To KNOW and LOVE

The mystery of being here:
Why? Why?
To know and love
the Creator, first of all,
and to show that love
in all we do
with all we contact
and, thereby,
civilization
will continue
and progress
for ever more.
It is not ourselves
to work for,
but the other,
and we will benefit
in the effort
here or after.

The WAY

Can we trust?
Trust the Force
that is Love
that sustains us.
Trust that no matter
the present pain
the end will be good.
It is all good,
for we gain
though this moment
we only see pain.
In pain we grow
and growth
is our reason.
Embrace the pain,
through tribulation
is our slavation –
for we ripen.

ADVANCE

The time is right,
the hour is dawn,
the days are not so long.

When will we know
what has been done
for the Kingdom to be won?

The desert is receding now,
the life within's begun,
and mankind will be one.

SOULS JOURNEY

The Ocean collects
drops, lost, wayward:
alone they don't know...
The pull of the Ocean
is strong, stronger
than other forces.
The drops travel,
some in groups,
others alone,
all to the Ocean –
their Source
and Reunion.
In the Ocean they merge
finding collictive bliss
now aware of oneness
they otherwise lacked.
Ocean is reunion
and restoration.

LIGHT Upon LIGHT

Beings of Light
connected by Love,
this,
true human nature.
To love and be loved
the basis
of our creation –
reason for existence.
More and more learn
this fundamental fact
of our existence.
Light reaches out
to Light and joins
even more Light
and together
radiate Love
to all existence
forevermore.

POWER

Taken from individuals
who abuse it
and given
to councils
of those elected
by their peers
as best qualified
and most detached
from the passions
of the times
for the benefit
of all
in their charge
for transformation
of the social fabric
of our lives
and hearts
and planet.

The WORD Which

The Day-Star of Thy Word,
shining….
above horizon.
Through a word of Thy mouth,
the word which split,
hath revolutionized
and divided
all creation,
through which
all things expire,
yet some
endued with new Life!
Thy most exalted Word,
the Divine Elixir
which transmutes
crude human life
into
purest gold!

REALITIES

Flying down the freeway
midst towering buildings –
speed, lights:
American hurry
with santour notes dancing
and chanted prayers
One wonders:
which world is real?
Do they merge and combine
influencing the other?
One gives the form,
the other the spirit?
Is there a balance –
form and spirit harmonized?
Until harmony is visible
I will pray and teach
and do my utmost
for transformation.

SPECK ARISING

One moving Speck of Dust
setting out alone
with angels for companions
to raise aloft the banner,
midst a hostile world,
of Beauty, Glory, Light,
to help transform
thirsty, yearning souls
and give them wings of flight.
"That ye may achieve,
this I cannot do –
How utterly I deplore it,"
was His ardent prayer.
The call of victory rings
across prairies, hills,
valleys and the seas,
as deserts bloom:
a world transforming.

PIONEERS for PEACE

Going to a land
    far from home
to live and work
    and end your days
building ties
    of understanding and respect
across cultures
    and political divisions;
this is a path
    towards peace:
a path taken
    by countless lovers
of humanity
    and peace –
little acts
    of ordinary folk
are essential for
    global transformation.

TEMPLE and the MOON

Shining bright,
the Temple and the moon,
lighting the Night,
showing the way
by their own Light
for travelers in the Night.
God created both
in His own way
guiding those
who wish to know.
The Temple and the moon,
exquisite jewels
of Divine Perfection,
symbols of more
than Earth can hear,
teaching beyond time,
through time
guiding to eternity.

SILENT TOMB

Silent, reverent tomb
filled with Light
upon Light,
and Roses.
For the One Denied
even a candle,
now rests eternally
amid Light.
Pilgrims come, pray,
cry tears of relief –
some are touched
deeper than they once
would have believed –
depart transformed.
Worlds converge
in this sacred
holy spot
forevermore.

FEAST of NÚR

Liberation, celebration:
    release.
"We are moving to Mazra'ih."

The gates of Akka open,
    pilgrims then pour in.
The Most Great Prison empties.

Jubilation: a centenary,
    a cycle now complete.
The Wheel of God has turned.

Kings have fallen, kingdoms vanished.
    The war to end all wars...
a beginning.

Jubilation, celebration;
    "the world of the soul,"
now restored, to the King.

The Feast of Núr, 135 B.E.
    prayers, papers and reports,
with tea and cookies.

WHEELS of TIME

The wheels that turn so slow,
we never see them go.

Our lives are small
so small,
we don't see them at all.

Unless, by chance,
we happen on a spot
that marks a cycle –
complete.

The Hundred Years of an Era:
the centennial of the Herald
the centennial of the Revelation,
the centennial of the Declaration,
the centennial of the Covenant.

Massive cycles of time –
all complete,
fulfilled,
and finished.

So slowly they turn,
so fully they become,
so majestic...
we cannot see.

Our lives are small,
so small,
we don’t see them at all,
yet note each turn
in its time.

NINE

19 Mercy – Another month has ended, where does the time go?

7 Words – Someday I'll get it all down. I will, I will. I know I will!

12 Words – Do I really have to put up with his babble all day long? Why can't he say something intelligent once in a while?!? Silence. I'd like a little silence.

4 Perfection – I can't say I've improved a whole lot, but I've stopt frowning when she comes into the room. I've begun trying to imagine, when I see her, how she might have looked as a little girl. That has helped a lot.

14 Perfection – I don't intend to write here everyday. That's not the goal. Just once in a while is enough – and not about what I do, as much as what I think!

9 Names – Tommy, Roya and Hashim. Bobby, Lua and Corinne. Rafiq, Rahim and Rae. We were all here.

2 Might – A windstorm came through last night and blew down the old tree on the corner. It had become rotten inside though it hadn't looked like it from the outside. Some people are like that – look good on the outside, but really are rotten on the inside and have no intergrity.

16 Might – It was difficult and I could have let it pass, but it wasn't right so I stood up and did not let the bully take advantage

of me. She was surprised and backed down suddenly. I was scared but stood my ground and I'm glad I did!

7 Will – I finally finished cleaning out the closet. I've intended to do that for months and got it done today. What a relief!

A KING with GLORY

In Samoa
  “we are all kings,”
said the Malietoa,
  the King,
seeing the nobility
  of his people,
and all people,
  as one.
The oldest,
  and longest reigning
monarch of the world –
  he was Bahá’í.
He elevated Samoa
  to a Point of Light
among the nations,
  no matter
if they were unaware:
  awareness will come.

VISITORS to FEAST

Not invited, unexpected,
  unwanted:
BIRDS!
  accidentally, unintentionally,
flying into the room
  from the fireplace chimney!
Panic! Screams!
  People jumping!
The birds wanted out
  and
people wanted them out,
  but how to help them...
Open the outside door!
  Shut the inside doors!
Amazingly –
  they flew out.
Calm restored,
  prayers resumed.

WINTER Of the WORLD

In the winter of the world
  frozen hearts and minds
are everywhere
  cruelty and ignorance.
The soft, sweet breeze
  of understanding,
acceptance and compassion
  is too seldom found
in the workings of the world
  and minds.
The warm light of knowledge
  does not pierce
cold darkness
  of frozen hearts,
yet Spring will come,
  souls will blossom
and the Earth
  will be made new.

MIRRORS of THEIR MINDS

In a city by the bay
  where the tide
comes and goes
  in eternal rhythm,
come lovers
  of a greater rhythm
that is eternal
  also,
the rhythm of The Message
  to the problems
of the world
  far and wide;
come they,
  consult, and go forth
to practice,
  implement new methods,
from a new perspective
  to change the world.

CONVOCATION of ILLUMINED SOULS

From far and near
they have come
to a gathering of minds
and hearts and souls,
to focus intellect and spirit
on regeneration
of social order
and purpose.
These are the lovers
of humankind,
who give of their lives
and self
with confidence that
the social fabric
of the world
CAN be re-created.
This is the purpose,
this is the joy!

I ASK

Have mercy on my soul,
Dear God, PLEASE!
I have tried,
only You know
how long and how hard
I have been trying.
Please, God forgive
my stupidities and self
absorbed times
when I could have done more.
I am sorry,
I beg You, God,
the All-Merciful, to forgive
this weak soul of mine.
I will try and I will fail,
but I pray
that I will learn
and fail less often.
Please God,
I beg Thee
with Thine aid
and assistance
I can improve
and grow stronger,
more mature, detached
and wise.
Make of me, O God,
a hollow reed
that I may show

Your Glory all around.
Please God,
let it be so.
I ask in Thy Name,
the All-Glorious,
the All-Forgiving,
the All-Merciful.

The SEARCH

Searching through centuries
  of beliefs and actions,
weighing them all
  in a heart
purified by pain
  for truth.
From ancient Sumerians
  to modern Mormons,
the seeker read and read
  and prayed.
With faint hope
  after years of search,
he wondered if ever
  he would find
the solace of his heart
  and mind.
One day, without wavering,
  he found Glory!

The WORD is ONE

Giving His sermon on the mount
Muhammad took a breath
and uttered timeless words.

Jesus stood in command
at the head of the army
to fight the true, inner jihad.

Jerusalem rang its bells
as Krishna rode the stallion
on the first of Ramadan.

The Gate of Glory opened
while drums and symbols
praised the Lord of Hosts.

Minarets of Byzantium sang
as Buddah raised His pen
and wrote immortal hymns.

Zoroaster strode the water
to launch Salvations Ark
upon the Sea of Self.

And the Word is One!

The BABY KNOWS

The baby crawls across the street;
  for there is little traffic
in this small town,
  and he is not afraid.
His mother cannot change
  his diaper or her habits
and his sister is in school,
  so he goes alone
when he needs help
  trusting
the people who are there –
  he knows will care.
They are always nice;
  some come and go,
and often feed him
  for there is always food
and kindness in action –
  Bahá'ís at their Center.

SEARCHING to the ENDS...

Searching high and low –
in field and forest,
over plains and seas,
over marsh and mountain,
where is that
which will fill my soul?
"...if thou searchest the universe
forever more,
they quest
will be in vain."
What...
will make me whole?
"...thou mayest find Me
standing within thee,
mighty, powerful
and self-subsisting."
Within my heart
all this time!

DECISION

You did What?!?
I changed the way to live my life.
But why?
Because it seemed a better way, more hopeful.
Better? Hopeful? The world's falling apart! Can't you see?
It is not all falling apart, that is only the outward sign of transition.
What transition?
From ways of doing centered on self or privilege, to ways that nurture souls.
What?!?
Motivation for limited interest, no longer works. That is against the needs of our time.
You're talking gibberish!
What works best, and is longer lasting, are decisions where all involved participate.
All – who?
All members of the human race who live with us on planet Earth.
What does that mean?
It means I'm part of a community of nurturing people with a purpose greater than all of us. I share that purpose now, and feel connected to every other one who is breathing on the planet.
And you think this is good?
It's more than good – it's Glorious!!

The SEAL of HATE

Trees fall
as a cyclone of hate
sweeps the land;
hate based on
limitations
of finite minds.
One word:
"seal,"
can mean many things:
certify (the truth),
verify (reality),
close and end (the prophets).
Choose the meaning
to gain the most hate.
And they have.
Hate.
Kill,
Destroy... Bahá'ís.

TAKE YE COUNSEL

"Take ye counsel together..."
 for problems large or small
together, minds and hearts
 can find solutions
after prayer and sincere
 deliberation.
All aspects can be seen
 from different points of view
with no credit or attachment
 to the information offered;
a solution is the goal
 based on principles and facts.
Insolvable dilemmas
 melt away
in the consultative process
 and new methods
to solve old problems
 will make this world anew!

IN THEIR HONOR

Fabricated crimes
  false accusations
imaginary charges
  welled from ignorance,
and today
  will be held
a pretentious trial
  to convict those
who have faith
  to their deaths!

A grasp of desperation
  to hold to superstition
as the world moves on
  by the Hand of God
to a new paradigm
  of understanding
and embrace
  of all the human race.

PRAYER FORCE

A single prayer grows
and is joined by others
and soon a chorus
of praise is wafting
over land and sea,
hills and plains,
and sometimes mountains
of ignorance and hate
are moved
and fellowship takes place.
Prayer has more power
and force when unified
than materialists
will allow.
Prayer
transforms the world.
"O God!
Let hearts be opened wide!"

NEW PROCESS

I give up an idea,
    you give up an idea,
he gives up an idea,
    she gives up an idea:
we all give up an idea
    to the group.

Every idea is examined
    by the group,
some are rejected,
    some are kept,
some are transformed
    and adapted.

Consultation continues,
    a decision begins to grow
and take shape
    before our inward eyes
and soon there stands
    a new decision for us all.

HASTEN, THOU

"Hasten...
that thou mayest
become
an
immortal soul."

Hasten –
do not tarry
on the earthly
plane,
your destiny
is nobler.

Hasten,
flee this life,
your role is brief
yet
significant,
necessary
and loved.

HOUSE of the FATHER

The House of the Father
  now destroyed
was lamented
  by the ignorant
who saw only
  their culture
destroyed
  by greater ignorance.

In time
  it will be rebuilt,
home of Mirza Buzurg,
  as a gift and heritage
to those who do not know
  the meaning of return.

In time,
  in God's own time,
it will,
  it shall, be done.

The MARVEL of UNION

Two strangers meet
  and find
    they are not strangers.

From two cultures,
  with alien traditions,
    they discover union.

The language of the heart
  is greater than
    the differences of words.

Union is astonishment
  differences arc minor,
    incidental.

It is the Spirit that unites;
  the Spirit
    of New Revelation.

The Revelation of Bahá
  grants new avenues
    of knowing and being.

New friends quickly
  become astonished
    at their oneness.

'There is a power
 in this Cause
  far beyond the ken

of men and angels…'
 the power of the beauty
  of Bahá.

JOHN ROGER WHITE

Poetic voice
   of a generation,
exploding
   sky rockets:
poems,
   songs of our heart
singing
   what we did not know
to say ourselves.

NEW HOLY SPACES

Around the Earth
new spaces are constructed
to create new levels
of unity and oneness,
a new social base
to allow awareness
that we are all
one family:
Nine sided forms
with domes
House of Light and Praise,
new sacred space
to welcome all
here, there, more and more
till all the world around
there will appear
holy spaces new
for all humanity.

GLIMMERING HOUSE

A painting, it appeared,
  but more – a vision:
memory has not faded
  three decades and more.
Shimmering pastels dance,
  sing of Glory, exaltation:
home of the Promised King,
  source of revelation
the Most Holy Book of Laws,
  laws for future civilizations,
on display a special exhibit
  shimmering on the wall
as if translucent glass
  radiant with light
co-joining glimpse of Heaven
  and majestic revelation:
House of ‘Abbud, transcendent,
  scintillating on the wall.

LIFE PAIN

Searing pain
right through the heart
purifies, they say,
a person's soul.
At the time
that's not believed –
it hurts so much!!!
But perspective:
days, months or years,
proves it true.
But why, oh why, oh why
does it hurt so much!!
Can't we learn
an easier way?
Is pain
the only effective path?
I do not,
do not understand.

EFFORT is…

Reaching, grasping
for truth, substance, reality
let it go
desire
the road, the path
faintly
not knowing but try
standing up
pushing on
unknown
but we will arrive
over the rainbow
when effort is sufficient.
No regrets
no lingering
we will succeed
courage
to carry on.

REFUGE of TREES

Protecting from the sun and heat
trees spread arms
high and wide over me
and sing
softly, gently, whispering –
I can sleep in peace.
On the prairie
precious trees,
a grove a treasure
along a creek
miraculously fed
by flowing spring.
One can forget here
unpleasant elsewhere
and dream:
someday
there will be Peace –
I will be free.

Co-WORKERS

Chaos and ruin
surround us.
Some make great effort
to destroy,
but call it restoration,
though it is only fantasy
they aim for.
Others make great effort
to truly destroy
and they often
loudly succeed.
Others, quietly
patiently
calmly
try and try and try
to build a new foundation
for further peace
and justice.

STRIVING HEARTS

Striving, striving
with hearts on fire
to build new
while living in
chaos of the old,
and destruction.
Some days
hopelessness abounds,
other days
Glory is amazing!
How sweet
success can be
when hearts turn
to their Beloved.
We try
and valiantly try –
eventual success
is assured.

The NAME

The Blessed Beauty
is the name
I prefer to use,
it speaks of Grandeur,
Glorious Perfection.
Yet, I know,
only hints at Reality
which none here
may see, but
some time beyond time
I will KNOW –
and Glory
will be all around
with praise and joy
for ever and ever and ever and ever!
Yá Bahá'u'l-Abhá!
Yá Bahá'u'l-Abhá!
Yá Bahá'u'l-Abhá!

ROSE BEAUTY

Rose –
blossom, scent, beauty:
Blessed Beauty.
Oh, my soul.
Faces – gorgeous
lit by love –
flower garden colors:
eyes sparkle
with delight,
teeth shine
in smiles.
Everywhere in the world
there is love, joy
and acceptance
of humanness:
perfection.
He, she, you,
and every other.

BREEZES of CERTITUDE

Flowers blooming
with fragrances of love
nodding in the breeze
of the Most Great Name.
Riḍván,
that Blessed Time
when time stands still
and creation
is renewed
for another season
and Glory to the Lord!
What days
compare to these
when certitude
is in bloom?
And joy…
pours forth
from every heart.

PARADISE of DAYS

The urgency of flowers
nodding in the wind
to say, “yes,”
and listen
as lace curtains,
blowing gently
between pillars,
invite the spirit
to soar
on words of love
and enchantment
on this holiest of holy
festivals of renewal,
resurrection,
and rebirth:
Riḍván, the Day
of Most Great Felicity
is HERE!

DIVINE SPRINGTIME

The Most Great Festival
Renewal
of Creation,
Divine Springtime:
Rebirth
and re-creating
all that is.
Potentials newly formed
planted
to be released
in time
to transform
and re-create
you
and me
in Divine Love
and Paradise
forevermore.

SPIRIT FLIGHT

Soaring as a bird
human soul
can fly
beyond human limits
when the soul
is not attached
to the earthly world
or allurements.
When a soul
is so detached
there is no limit,
earthly or other,
that can prevent
its soaring.
The challenge
is to fly
heedless of self
or desires.

MESSENGER of JOY

The Angel of Joy
came to me,
I was distracted,
wasn't ready.
So much…
was still undone,
so many plans…
unfulfilled –
But, no matter:
it was time
for me to leave.
How I wish
I had done
so much, much more.
But it was over
and I was free.
What joy
and joy and joy!

INDWELLING

You are in a cloud,
and yet,
you can see far.
There is nothing above you
or below you,
or anywhere around you:
just,
the cloud, which is not a cloud.
It is not a moisture cloud,
but tender, light, and loving.
Yes: loving.
The Cloud loves you.

And you rejoice;
you are exalted.
You feel as if joy is bursting
out of you in all directions.
Which it is.
Your joy becomes part of the joy
and love of the Cloud.

You are Joy
The Cloud is Greater Joy
and Love.

Without a sense of movement,
for there is nothing now to move,
you meet,
sometimes gather,

with others like yourself –
rejoicing in the Cloud.
Some, you recognize,
others ...
it does not matter.

There is no hunger, thirst or pain,
and no end.
The Glory endures forever,
and so now –
do you.

NOTES:

The Baby Knows: Based on the true experience of a child growing up across the street from the Lapiwa, Idaho Baha'i Center.

Breezes of Certitude: Riḍván, Paradise, name of a garden and twelve day period celebrating the declaration of Bahá'u'lláh of His Mission to the world.

Divine Springtime: "The Most Great Festival" refers to the Festival of Riḍván, see Breezes of Certitude.

House of the Father: This is the home of Mirza Buzurg, the father of Bahá'u'lláh, an exqusite example of period architecture destroyed by those wishing to erase all evidence of the Bahá'í Faith from Iran.

Messenger of Joy: "I have made death a messenger of joy to thee. Wherefore dost thou grieve? I made the light to shed on thee its splendor. Why dost thou veil thyself therefrom?" ~ Bahá'í scriptures.

The Name: "Yá Bahá'u'l-Abhá" meaning: "O Thou the Glory of Glories!" A prayer and invocation. See Rose Beauty for the meaning of 'Blessed Beauty.'

Nine: Partially fictional diary/journal entries using the Badí' calendar of the Bahá'í Faith.

Marvel of Union. This poem celebrates the friendship of Dr Hasan Shodiev, a native of Samarkand, Uzbekistan with the author. Dr Shodiev came to Kansas on a NATO grant to learn how to help his country. He wanted to stay longer than the grant would pay for, so the author offered to host him in his home. They had become friends before the grant ran out, but while living in the same house they became brothers. This development was a delight to both of them.

Observational: “Dost thou reckon thyself only a puny form when within thee the universe is folded?” ~ Bahá’í scriptures

“Turn thy sight unto thyself, that thou mayest find Me standing within thee, mighty, powerful and self-subsisting.” ~ Bahá’í scriptures

Open the Door: “Turn thy sight unto thyself, that thou mayest find Me standing within thee, mighty, powerful and self-subsisting.” ~ Bahá’í scriptures

“Love Me, that I may love thee. If thou lovest Me not, My love can in no wise reach thee. Know this, O servant.” ~ Bahá’í scriptures

Paradise of Days: See Riḍván.

Ridván: Paradise, name of a garden and twelve day period celebrating the declaration of Bahá’u’lláh of His Mission to the world.

Rose Beauty: “Blessed Beauty,” a title of Bahá’u’lláh, the Glory of God, Prophet-Founder of the Bahá’í Faith.

Speck Arising: “O that I could travel, even though on foot and in the utmost poverty, to these regions, and, raising the call of “Ya Bahá’u’l-Abhá” in cities, villages, mountains, deserts and oceans, promote the divine teachings! This, alas, I cannot do. How intensely I deplore it! Please God, ye may achieve it.” ~ ‘Abdu’l-Bahá (Head of the Bahá’í Faith, 1892-1921)

To Know and Love: “I bear witness, O my God, that Thou hast created me to know Thee and to worship Thee.” ~ Bahá’í scriptures

Credits

Open the Door – Tiferat Anthology of Spiritual Poems

The Word is One – Ichnographical: 173

Hasten, Thou – Praise the King of Glory

INDEX of FIRST LINES

www.ingramcontent.com/pod-product-compliance
Ingram Content Group UK Ltd.
Pitfield, Milton Keynes, MK11 3LW, UK
UKHW041821200726
13854UKWH00001BA/434

9 789395 224062